16/10/2018

Katheryn,
Enjoy the memories

THE CRANE

TOM HENEGHAN

Tom Heneghan

16/10/2018

DRAWINGS: KATRINA MAGUIRE

TYPESETTING: MARTIN HENEGHAN

PRINTING: HENEGHAN PRINTERS
                     135A RICHMOND ROAD
                     DUBLIN 3

ISBN: 0-9539613-0-3

PUBLISHED 2000 BY: TOM HENEGHAN
PHONE: (01) 8417294   MOBILE: 087 7737729
          Email: tomhany@yahoo.co.uk

CONTENTS

BIRTH

It was the 7th October 1947.
The feast day of the Holy Rosary.
The venue was Castlebar Hospital.
The nurse said: "IT'S A BOY!"
The end of life in the womb.
The start of a new adventure.
A new life in a new World.
And in Ireland at that.
What's it all about?
Better make the most of it.
I'll have a little cry first though.
35,674 of us boys were born in Ireland
that year.
The number of girls was 33,304.
And they say there's more women in the
World than men.
My uncle Martin passed away to a new life
a few weeks before I was born.
He was just 27 years of age.
Life is like an airport; one departing
and one arriving.
The most popular song of 1947 was: '0 What
a Beautiful Morning'.
Frankie Lane was the most popular singer.
The most popular musical was 'Finians Rainbow'.
It was the year of the big snow.

New York was the venue for the 1947
All-Ireland Football Final.
Cavan beat Kerry, in Gaelic Park, by
2-11 to 2-7.
Kilkenny beat Cork by 0-14 to 2-7 in the
Hurling Final at Croke Park.
Across the Irish Sea 'Charlton' won the
F.A. Cup in England.
Over to Beechers Brook and the Grand
National was won by 'Caughoo'.
Anyone for tennis?
Jack Kramer won the Wimbledon Tennis
tournament.
The Ladies winner was Margaret Osborne.
St. Peters Chair in Rome was occupied by
Pope Plus XII. in 1947.
Harry Truman was President of the United
States of America.
The British Prime Minister was
Clement Attlee.
Sean T. O'Kelly was President of Ireland.
The Taoiseach was Eamonn De Velera.
1947 saw India gain her Independence, and
a new Israeli State was emerging.
In the midst of all these happenings a
new life is born.
WOW!

YOUR OWN MEMORIES

_____

_____

_____

_____

_____

_____

_____

_____

_____

_____

_____

_____

_____

_____

_____

_____

_____

_____

_____

NAN

My oldest brother, Pa, started to call my
Mother Nan when he was small.
The name stuck, so Nan it is.
Though some may call her May.
She'd sweep the hearth when she had got the
others out to school.
Then she'd sit down and smoke a woodbine.
Bridgie May, May McHugh, or Bridie Ruane
might call.
They'd talk and laugh; laugh from the heart.
Then we'd go to the well.
Up the shaded boreen to the hill.
Viewed by an odd cow chewing the cud.
Down the steps into a round opening in
the ground.
Filled our bucket with pure clear spring water.
Long before Ballygowen was heard of.
Brod Staunton stops to share a joke.
We'd take a rest now and then on the return
journey, and pick an odd flower.
A may flower, a primrose, a daisy or a bluebell.
"Whose field is that in there", I'd say to Nan.
"John Bodkins", she'd say.
"THAT FIELD IN THERE", I'd say.
"John Bodkins", she'd say.
A four year old making doubly sure.

She'd bring me to Mass, in Belcarra, on the
carrier of the bike.
"Keep your legs out from the spokes",
I was warned.
All I'd see was the road going back behind me
as we edged our way to the chapel.
We'd hear the sound of clop, clop, clippity
clop in the distance.
"That's Cannons horse and trap", says Nan.
The clippity clops got louder and louder.
With waving passengers the horse and trap
eased its way past us.
The chapel bell mingled with, and then faded
out the clippity clops.
A bar of chocolate for me after Mass.

Nan performed many a task.

Never a dull moment.
She'd feed the hens and collect the eggs.
Do the baking and do the washing.
She'd bake the spud cake and make
the porridge.
Light the fire and light the lamp.
She put us to bed and got us up.
Calmed our fears and dried our tears.
Plus a million other things and more.
I don't know how she passed her free time,
as there were only ten of us in it.
That's Nan and she was always there.

DA

He'd take us on turns in the van with him.
Each journey was a mystery tour for us
small ones.
You could find yourself in Mulranny
or Newport.
In Crossmolina or Lehardane.
Bohola, Kilkelly, Shrule, or Ballindine.
More often than not, however, it was back
the west.
We would stop and say hello to Tom Carty
in Ballintubber.
Have a chat with John Lally in Tourmakeady.
Drop in to Mick Walsh in Killawalla.
Get a bite to eat in Malones of Westport.
On then to Da's favourite place:
Drummin at the foot of Croagh Patrick.
The kettle was always on the boil in Mrs.
Berrys house.
"Will we have the tae now, or will we wait
until we come over", says Da.
"Arragh we'll have it now", says Tommy
And Mrs. Berry had it on the table anyway.
Tommy and Josie were ready to discuss
any subject.
"We went up the big hill looking for the
sheep", said Josie.

"We couldn't find one of them the fog was
so thick", said Tommy.
Walking Shaffrey hills in the dew of a
foggy morning.
"Let ye drink up the tea now before it goes
cold", said Mrs. Berry.
"Did ye climb the reek this year?", says I.
Just to say something ya know.
Berrys house nestles nicely at the foot of
the Holy mountain.
They say Drummin people are the salt of
the Earth.
"We'll go In the name of God", said Da, 'the
nights are gettin' short'.
So off we set back home to Donamona.
Da knew every highway and byway in Mayo.
Down twisty roads to discover who or what
was at the end.
At night as we fell asleep we'd hear the sound
of the van in the distance.
Another day over. Time to give the van
a rest.
The great bonfire was held on his feast day:
St. Johns day.
He always made it home before the fire
died down.
He'd lead us in prayer as we circled the
fading embers.

12

DONAMONA

Every morning we saw the old stooped man
in the distance.
Crossing wall after wall with the load of
hay on his back
Getting closer and closer until he reached
our house.
Then passing on up the boreen to his cattle.
Hail, rain, or snow he always appeared.
Then one morning he didn't appear.
Old age had caught up with him.
And we missed him.
It seemed a hard way to live life.
But might he not be happier than a King.
Just one memory of Donamona.
It's still a quiet place.
Quieter even than a few years ago.
Maddens shop is gone; with Annie, Paddy
and Freddie.
Gone too is 'The Fair Day of Donamona.'
It was a kind of moving fair.
It started off in Ryan's field.
Then gradually everything began to move in
procession towards the crossroads.
Carts, trucks, vans, cars, trailers, cattle and,
of course, people.
The fact that Tuffy's pub was at the cross
may have influenced this movement.

The ruins of the castle remind us that Donamona
was once a hive of activity.
Dún-na-Móna: (Fortress in the bog)
Parts of Mayo were governed from this castle.
It's hard to imagine Mayo being governed
from Donamona.
But it's all tranquil now.
"Nobody left at home now but the very old and
the very young" said Mary Loftus.
Forthlawn forth looks down on Donamona.
Croagh Patrick is peeping in the distance.
The famous twelfth century abbey of Ballin-
tubber is just back the road.
The old S.M.A. college of Ballinafad is
even closer over the road.
And Ballydavoc across the lakeeen.
The art of storytelling is dying out.
Walter Joyce (Senior) fulfilled that role
to a T for us.
He had his own corner beside our open
hearth fire.
And there was hushed silence as he recounted
the time his bicycle was stolen.
The peace and tranquillity of Donamona, or
the hustle and bustle of New York.
Which of the two would one choose?
Both 1 suppose.

Croagh Patrick is a mountain where St. Patrick is said to have preached. There is a statue at the ~~bottom~~ beginning of the path up to mountain where celebrations are held each year.

YOUR OWN MEMORIES

THE MILE TO SCHOOL

The Golden mile to Clogher school.
It wasn't always golden for us, but it had
its own characteristics.
Modern children miss the adventure of
walking to school.
But do they know that?
Stuck into a bus; maybe not as bad as being
a battery hen.
For seven years we walked that mile.
Sometimes alone with our little thoughts.
Sometimes with the crowd.
But always full of adventure.
What a wonderful way to experience the
four seasons.
The refreshing autumn winds with its
nostalgic feelings.
Walking through flashes of water with our
new wellingtons.
Then ploughing through mountains of leaves
blown down by the wind.
On into the colder darker days of winter.
The frost turning the little flashes of
water into ice.
Ideal conditions for us skiers.
We craved for snow; the icing on the cake
of winter.

Roll on Spring
New Life, new hope.
New buds, new flowers.
Everything bursting forth with joy.
Does the evergreen miss out by not dying?
Spring transforms itself into Summer.
Long hot days.
We discard our shoes.
Off to school in our feet.
All nature in full bloom now.
Accompanied by a full orchestra of bees
and birds.
Even the telegraph poles are humming.
Men Ploughing the land.
Saving the hay and cutting the oats.
Our mile to school started off, naturally,
at our gateeen.
Past Ballydavock boreen.
Up the hill and round the turn
Down the other side past Joe Blowicks.
On to the straight stretch, and past the
green boreen.
Round the turn, and another one at
Ned Roaches.
Round two more turns and past Guilfoyles.
Round the last turn, past Scahills boreen
Finally over the little Pebble river, and there
stood our school.

SCHOOL DAYS

'Those were the days my friend
We thought they'd never end'.
But they did!
Our teacher said: "They'll go in spite of ye".
"The best days of your life", some told us.
We had our doubts.
Neither the best nor the worst I suppose.
Just school days.
I asked for my lunch the moment I arrived
for my first day at school.
Signs of trauma setting in.
We served our time in the Missesus room before
we graduated into the Masters.
Missesus was a word invented by us newcomers.
We sat two to a very heavy desk.
Everything was heavy in those days.
That was before our throw away
everything era.
Each desk had two little ink wells.
But we weren't allowed touch them yet.
Could you imagine if we were?
We had to satisfy ourselves with marla.
Marla was the best thing ever invented as
far as we were concerned.
With it we made all kinds of everything.

Time to move on out into the
Masters room.
"I love this Jimin", said the Master,
during the Irish class.
He knew, and we knew that he knew,
that we didn't.
"Get up to the blackboard, Heneghan,
and do that sum".
It wasn't my favourite place to be.
'Stand ye now for Erins glory', began the
Master, for no particular reason.
'Stand ye now for Erins cause', we all joined
in in chorus.
My grand-uncle, Tom Kilcourse, was a teacher
in the old school in the 1930's.
Teasie's father that would be.
Every family brought a cart load of
turf to school.
It kept the Clogher school fires burning.
There was a small round hole in the
wooden floor.
Maybe put there by the builder remembering
his own school days.
That little hole devoured every cane when
the Master was out.
The school days passed in spite of us,
by the way.

YOUR OWN MEMORIES

NAN DOWN IN GUESDIAN

She was our Granny but we called her 'Nan
down in Guesdian' for short.
She lived with her son Miko.
I'd cycle down to see her
Down the boreen amongst the trees.
The green fields and little hilleens.
Life was tranquil there.
A little Paradise.
No television, no radio.
Just one with nature.
The apple trees stood on the hilleen
behind the back door.
The perfume of a little rose bush greeted
you outside the front door.
There was a callach beside the fireplace.
Always a nice fire in the big open-hearth.
The kettle singing away.
There she sat beside the fire.
Always believing, hoping and smiling.
Resignation to God's will.
Miko loved his brown loaf and tea, and he
had lots of jokes.
Why did the penny stamp?
Because the three-penny-bit.
One of his old money jokes.

Granny always washed the cup in the saucer
before she'd give you the tea.
And it was washed already.
Time for me to be getting restless.
'Don't be rumegin there', she'd say.
I'd be rootin' through the dresser to see what
I could find.
The Far-East magazine was always there.
She'd send me to Belcarra on the bike
for flannelette.
"Suppose they haven't got it", says I.
"They'll have it, they'll have it", came the
positive reply.
And they did indeed.
I'd help Miko drive the ass and cart.
Help may not be the appropriate word.
But Miko made it look as if I was
helping him.
Time to be going home after a busy day.
"Good bye granny, I'll be back again to help
out next week".
Away I go on the bicycle.
Once I passed the graveyard I was O.K.
Then one day Granny passed away.
On to a higher plane.
And we'll visit her some day.
Nan up in Guesdian.

THE TARRING OF OUR ROAD

It was like Cape Cinaverel outside
our house.
Our road being tarred for the first time.
Machines, all shapes and sizes, on
our doorstep.
We had never seen the likes before.
We had seen a corn thresher alright
on a few occasions.
And listened to its beautiful
humming sound.
We had watched as the ESB men erected
the heavy poles.
'High-Hup' they went as they lifted each
pole with their backs.
As a result everything was brightened
up by electricity.
But now we were thrown headlong into
the 20th. century.
First to arrive was the green caravan.
Here the foreman made his home for
a few weeks.
Next came the crusher which broke stones
into all shapes and sizes.
Along comes the steam-roller which makes
everything stay down.

Workmen and their shovels, everywhere.

We all played our part too.

We didn't stand idly by.

Nan had the water on the boil for the
workmens tea.

We, wee ones, helped to light the coloured
lights to warn passers-by.

Like the house lamps they had paraffin oil,
a wick, and a globe.

The place had a Christmas look about
it at night.

We didn't refuse either when invited into
the foremans caravan.

After weeks of putting everything in place
the big moment arrived.

The tarring machine was here and our road
would never be the same again

'Keep back there men', said the ganger,
'that's dangerous'.

Men with shovels of chippings followed
the tarring-machine.

The steam-roller had the final say.

A job well done, but a sadness on our part.

All the noise and activity had departed for
another area.

The familiar dusty old road gives way to
the smooth new one.

A time of change is upon us.

CLIMBING THE REEK

'Croagh Patrick' it's known as universally.
But to us locals it's 'The Reek'.
'Are you going to the Reek?'
The question was often asked coming up
to Reek Sunday.
Finally my turn came; I was ten.
'Would my young fella there be able to
climb it?' asked Da.
'Ah sure he'll run up it', came the reply.
I was indeed relieved.
The big night arrived.
The climb started at midnight.
Two hours to the summit.
'Sticks for the Reek', shouted a man as
we were about to ascend.
We had provided our own.
It was dark and wet, but we just followed
the crowd.
'Are we near the top', says we.
'Just around the next corner', came a
reply out of the dark.
But there were quite a lot of corners
to go yet.
Lots of jokes passed between those going
up and those coming down.
Prayerful humour prevailed.

Quarter way up we circled Saint
Patrick's statue.
Little lights in the hazy distance coming
from the minerals tents.
The humble donkey was ideal for carrying
up the load.
He felt fulfilled I hope.
The top section of the mountain is almost
straight up.
We reached the misty summit.
After circling the little chapel we
participated at Mass.
A refreshing wind blowing through the
large crowd.
As it had done for fifteen centuries.
St. Patrick ordered the snakes out of
Ireland from here.
Time to negotiate the tricky descent.
As dawn breaks the view is breathtaking.
Clew Bay amongst the white clouds.
The little islands sitting pretty on the
Atlantic Ocean.
Tir-na-Nog is out there somewhere.
Wearily reaching the bottom now.
'Are we near the top', shouts someone
starting his climb.
'Ah, just around the next corner', says we.
One of my dreams fulfilled.

YOUR OWN MEMORIES

OUR FIRST RADIO

Our first radio was a big affair.
Large enough for the man to sit behind to
read out the news.
It had a glass battery full of acid.
I sometimes carried it to town, on the bike,
to get it charged.
Too much like work, so we put our
scientific minds to work.
We used a flashlamp battery instead.
We were in touch with the outside World
for the first time.
Our only contact with a radio before that was
in a neighbours house.
A crowd of us gathered, in Deacys, to listen to a
football match.
Everybody all ears.
Complete silence followed by a roar
after a score.
Our independence was established with
our very own radio.
We could pick and choose what we wanted
to listen to.
We woke up every morning to the sound
of O'Donnell Abu.
Radio Eireanns opening signature tune
of the day.

We had 'The Boys from the County Armagh' for
breakfast on Saturday morning.
Sung by Bridle Gallagher on the 'Cidona'
programme.
Michael P. O'Connor gave us the story of
'Wimple and Womple' after school.
The 'Top 20' on Radio Luxembourg passed
Sunday evenings for us.
A piano tune called 'Side Saddle' reached
no. 1 on one occasion.
Played excellently by Ross Conway.
Tom Foley ended up tying himself in knots
on the 'Foley Family'.
We tried to answer all of Joe Linnanes
questions on 'Question Time'.
We knew everything of the happenings of the
'Kennedys of Castleross'.
We followed the antics of 'Christy' with his
mother Maureen Potter.
Sean O'Morchu greeted us with a Cead Failte
Romhat on 'Teach-a Ceili'.
We often 'Took the Floor' with Dinjo in
the evenings.
We had 'Sports Stadium' on Saturday and
Michael O'Hehir on Sunday.
Then Waltons last word from Leo McGuire:
'If you feel like singing, do sing an
Irish song'.

COME ON TO THE BOG

'Come on to the bog', says Da.
The month was April.
Words often repeated over the summer.
We developed a dislike for those words
because they meant work.
Anyway off we set for Kilboyne bog on a
beautiful Spring morning.
The gentle breeze carrying the smell of
the heather towards us.
'Good morning Ned', says Da to our
bank-of-turf neighbour.
Ned was a man of few words, and always
kept his patch neat and tidy.
The turf was cut with a slan.
Then spread with a fork or wheelbarrow.
It was left for a few days when it was
turned and footed.
A few days later it was re-footed.
There it was left for a couple of weeks.
Then Neidin, the donkey, took it to the
roadside to be stacked.
The bog was a hive of activity during
the summer.
Everybody as busy as a bee.
It was like Indian territory at times.

Little columns of smoke rising up from
all areas of the bog.
It was lunch time and the fir-Gortha was
creeping over us.
After boiling the water for the tea down
go the eggs.
As the bog is such a hungry place two each
was no problem.
Now and then we took breaks between breaks
if Da wasn't looking.
We sank into the heather and watched the lark
soar higher and higher.
Whistling his own unique song as he rose.
Then swooping down and disappearing
in the heather.
Jumping the trenches was another
favourite passtime.
Finally Da would say: 'We'll go in the
name of God'.
It was like music to our ears after a hard
day of breaks.
We wandered in to see Ned and Sarah before
we departed.
Sarah did most of the talking as she
made the tea.
Her melodic voice sighing the future.
Yeah, the bog community may be no more.

YOUR OWN MEMORIES

MEN NOW

We stood at Frenchhill Hall, for a break,
with our bicycles.
Making our way to secondary school for
the very first time.
We didn't know we were leaving our
childhood behind.
Maybe we weren't yet.
After a pause off we set again.
It was the beginning of the swinging 60's.
So people informed us later on.
What would the future bring?
Our mode of transport is the bicycle.
A great little instrument.
It carried us the eight miles, hail, rain
or snow, to town and back.
Wonderful exercise too.
Whistling a tune as we cycled along.
We reached the town of Castlebar.
It could have been New York.
Round by the Mall and down Market Square.
Safely arrived we headed into a new room
with a new smell.
Complete silence as the Care-Taker walked
through the class to open a window.
We thought it was the Head-Master.

Eventually the Head-Master did stand in
front of us.
'Good morning boys and girls'.
He gazed at us in silence before he
spoke again.
'You are no longer little children'.
I'm sure he had his doubts.
'You are embarking on a new adventure at
this stage of your life'.
We looked around the room at each other.
'We wish you success in your time spent
here at this school'.
'What you make of it depends on you'.
Dramatic words.
Lunch time was spent exploring the town
of Castlebar.
We strolled through Main Street on a
daily basis.
Down Castle Lane too for an ice-cream
cone, and a macaroon bar.
Such adventure!
Took a walk now and then through the
green Mall.
We stood on the corner too watching all
the girls go by.
My mind wanders to Joe and Maureen just
starting in Clogher N.S.
Bye, bye childhood.

THE TWO JOHNS

They were in most Irish homes together.
In a framed picture above the mantlepiece.
The two Johns and the Sacred Heart.
Pope John XXIII and President John
Fitzgerald Kennedy.
The World seemed O.K. in their hands.
Pope John was old in years, but young
in Spirit.
Being 77 when elected some saw him
as an interim Pope.
Somebody who would not rock the boat.
He started the second Vatican Council.
As he said: 'To open the windows, and let
in some fresh air'.
It turned out to be a storm, and how the
boat was rocked.
People still trying to calm the waters.
The storm being caused more by others reaction
than by his actions.
He said the church is a garden to be cultivated,
not a monument to be preserved.
He retained his simplicity to the end.
He was warm-hearted and good-humoured.
The best way to salt life.
John XX111 the Good Pope.

The other John was elected to the White House
around the same time.
The youngest President of the U.S.up to now.
A Catholic, with a broad smile, of
Irish descent.
Like Pope John he brought a freshness to
peoples lives.
'Ask not what your country can do for you, but
what you can do for your country'.
Everyone remembers those famous words.
He came over to find his roots in Wexford.
Drank a cup of tea, with his cousins,
in the Garden.
One of our own.
On leaving he said he'd come back in
the Springtime.
But a different destination awaited him
in the Autumn.
Leaving Jackie a young widow.
'Where were you when you heard of his
assassination in Dallas, Texas?'
Coincidentally, or maybe not, both Johns
died the same year.
Pope John XX111 died on 3rd. June 1963
President John Fitzgerald Kennedy died on
the 22nd. November 1963.
We know not the day nor the hour, for the
plucking of the flower.

THE BEETLE AND THE BEATLES

Both the Beatles and the Beetle burst onto
the scene at the same time.
The Beatles came from England, and the
Beetle came from Germany.
Sounds awfully creepy-crawly.
Henry Ford took centre stage in Ireland
for a long while.
The Volkswagen Beetle arrived, so Ford
took a back seat.
Elvis Presley took centre stage at that
time also.
Four Liverpool Lads arrived and the young
went wild with Beatlemania.
Cathal Duffy was the V.W. livewire on the
local, Castlebar, scene.
He employed me, so I knew the Beetle
part by part.
I supplied the mechanics who serviced
the Beetle.
'Two oil filter gaskets there Tommy', was
the most frequent request.
The part number sounds as familiar as
ever: 113 115 189.
And the comment of the time on the
Volkswagen Beetle:
'Oh she's a very reliable car'.

While the Beatles were famous World-wide
we had our local heroes.
The Showband scene was here.
Brendan Bowyer jumped six feet off the
stage with the 'Hucklebuck'.
Dickie Rock went from the 'Candy-store on
the Corner' to the Chapel on the hill.
Eileen Reid gave her 'Wedding Dress' away.
Larry Cunningham took us through
'Lovely Leitrim'.
That was our Sunday night scene.
Dancing away the hours in the large ballrooms.
The hair plastered with brylcream.
"Where'll we go tonight lads?"
"Oh, to the Royal in Castlebar."
"No, we'll go to the Lakeland in Pontoon."
"What about Tooreen?"
"Sure we're always goin' there."
We arrived somewhere anyway.
When all else failed we had our local Arcadia
ballroom in Belcarra.
We had our local, Brose Walsh, band too.
Possibly the first Showband; founded in 1937.
My uncle Tom played with the band, in Frenchill,
on their first performance.
Brose himself has now passed on, but the
band plays on.
Memories are made of this.

YOUR OWN MEMORIES

_____

_____

_____

_____

_____

_____

_____

_____

_____

_____

_____

_____

_____

_____

_____

_____

_____

_____

_____

_____

_____

_____

BELCARRA CHAPEL

The bells still rang out at dawn.
We still had to turn sharp right at the forge
to reach the chapel.
But inside things were changing.
Vatican 2 made itself felt in our Parish
straight away.
The much-loved Fr. Gibbons had just left
for another Parish.
We missed his organ playing before Mass.
The new Priest began to face us.
Much more difficult for him I imagine.
There was a certain mystery attached to
the old way.
The Latin gave way to the native tongue.
Or in our case English.
As an alter boy I had a cupla fochail of
the Latin myself.
Fr. William Walsh fell in with the changes
straight away.
When not the celebrant he walked up and
down the aisle during Mass.
Explaining in detail all the new changes.
'He who prays will certainly be saved', I
heard him once quote.
He had a nice mixture of the modern
and conservative.

Coughing and nose blowing seemed an integral
part of the Latin days.
During the consecration a quietness fell upon
the congregation.
A deep acknowledgement of the people for the
sacredness of the moment.
Once It was over a great chorus of
coughing erupted.
It seemed to me the louder the nose blow the
more educated the person.
As well as the Liturgy our Chapel needed
an overhaul too.
Fr. William was the right man in the right
place to tackle that job also.
He loved working with stone.
Fr. Brendan navigates the Belcarra ship through
the millennium door
The Chapel is the main feature of the tidy
Belcarra village.
The Latin may be gone.
The altar rails may be gone.
Old ways give way to new ways.
Old structure replaced by new structure.
But the essential element of Belcarra Chapel
remains the same.
A place of worship and praise.
I rejoiced when I heard them say: 'Let us
go to Gods house'.

THREE IN A ROW

Galway were going for three in a row in
Connaught, and All-Ireland too.
However Mayo were ready to try and put
a spanner in the works.
The Connaught Football Final was about
to commence.
Cars parked along the side of the road for
miles outside Castlebar.
People converging on McHale Park from
all directions.
The pitch is as green as the green, green
grass of home.
In the distance Nephin mountain shows its
own colour of blue.
A Pipe-Band, forming a centrefield circle,
in all colours.
Playing 'Far away from the Land of the
shamrock and heather'.
And 'Galway Bay' too.
The roar of the crowd signals the arrival
of the teams.
Mayo in their green and red jerseys.
Galway in their maroon.
Flags of the same colours mingled
in the crowd.

"The ball is in and the game is on".
It's tit for tat.
Are Galway pulling away now though?
Oh no they're not, because Ruddy scores
a great goal for Mayo.
The roar could be heard in Achill.
Nothing in it at half time.
"How do you think it'll go Steve?"
"Galway'll take over in the second half
I reckon."
"Maybe, Steve, maybe not."
The second half battle is on.
"Ah will ya curl yer cue," came a shout
from the crowd.
My translation would be that he sent
the ball wide.
The game is almost over and the sides
are level again.
Galway, however, manage one last point.
The roar could be heard in Salthill
this time.
The final whistle blows.
Galway had achieved the three in a row in
Connaught, and All Ireland too.
A deep sadness descended on us Mayo folk.
Though it's better to have played and lost
than not to have played at all.
Is it not?

LEAVING THE NEST

I suppose it had to happen sometime.
To leave ones home behind.
I was lucky though.
I was already out of it before I realised the
enormity of leaving.
It struck me as I drove the Prinz car to
Castlebar station.
Leaving the familiar behind.
Brendan took full control of the Prinz after
I parked it in town.
I stood on the station platform.
Thoughts of past and future.
I wasn't fully in the present anyway.
The whistle of the train in the distance.
It's goodbye to Mayo now.
I passed my uncle Pat's house up the line.
Nestled among the Ballyshaun hills.
The train rolls on.
Through Manulla, Balla, Claremorris.
Through the Roscommon countryside.
I was really in orbit now.
No turning back at this stage.
I finally disembarked at Athlone station.
So far away from home.
(Just up the line, but don't tell anyone).

I settled into a little village called
Ballykeeran.
A beautiful mediterranean type hamlet.
With little hills, trees and lakes.
I made my home at St Pauls on the hill.
Looking down on the Post Office, the Mill,
the shop and the Dog & Duck.
The Bremesford river completes the picture.
I prayed morning and evening in the little
chapel at St.Pauls.
Spent the daytime hours on the offset
printing press.
I visited the Nuns across the road for a
chat now and again.
Played football with the local lads.
And drank a cup of tea with Jim, Sarah and
Frances at the gate lodge.
Athlone, on the river Shannon, was
now my town.
The town of the Musical Society and
Raymond Collins.
Everybody is unique, but Ray is more
unique than others.
He loves to entertain with his singing.
A Ray of hope maybe.
I myself was becoming a midlands man.
Bathed by the shannon breeze.

YOUR OWN MEMORIES

THE MOON

We ignore it most of the time.
Like a lot of things we take it
for granted.
But the Moon is always there.
It really shows its beauty on a
clear night.
When the curtains of cloud are
drawn back .
'Last week she was smaller and shaped
like a bow.
Now she's grown bigger and round as an O'.
It follows one around too.
I was in Italy once and there was the Moon
looking down.
Maybe the most familiar thing 1 could
see there.
Man decided to go to the Moon.
Wishful thinking some thought.
But in 1969, sure enough, off he goes.
The World held its breath.
Amazingly too we could watch the event
live on our own Planet.
'One small step for Man.
One giant leap for Mankind'.
Poetic words from Neil Armstrong as he
hopped on to the Moon.

'Wiser and weaker the generations will be',
I once heard my Mother say.
Landing on the Moon concentrated our minds
more on Earth too.
If we could walk on the Moon why not do a
better job on Earth.
Something to do with the spiritual side of
life I presume.
Anyway diversity brings a certain
spice to life.
While the rocket headed moonwards some
couldn't start their cars.
While Aldwin dug the moondust the Arigna
men were digging for coal.
Somebody said the Moon is a child
of the Earth.
A child who shines her light.
Of course she has her cloudy moments
like all of us.
However she always breaks through shining
as bright as ever.
And the cycle continues.
Birth as a bow, full bloom as an O and death
as another bow.
What are the chances of the man in the Moon
paying us a visit?
If he can get the spaceship started
who knows.

ITALY

'What am I doing here', says I to myself
in my own mind.
It was a big step from Donamona to Italy,
but here I was.
Sitting on the edge of a swimming pool in
the dusk of the evening.
Nobody about just me and my thoughts.
I was about to meet my group members to
enter novitiate.
The day before I had flown for the very
first time.
It was a wonderful experience with a mixture
of fear and excitement.
Looking down on the city lights of London
as we made our descent.
My brother, Sean, met me at Heathrow.
Next morning we set off for Gatwick airport
by train.
Through a maze of criss-crossing railway lines.
Up into the sky again from Gatwick.
Out over France and the snow-covered Alps.
Down by the 'thigh' of Italy to Rome;
at the 'knee'.
I descended at Ciampino airport, and boy
was it hot.
The Superior General was there to meet me.

Here I am in the Eternal City.
St Peters Square bathed in sunshine as
Pope Paul imparts his blessing.
The jaunting car is ready to take us to
the Coliseum.
Then on to the Catacombs and Tre Fontane.
I got a grasp of the Italian language
after a struggle.
Gennaro took me to the 'ankle' of Italy to a
little town called Vico.
Vico del Gargano is stuck into the side
of a mountain.
I had an early morning mirage there as
I looked out the window.
A procession of men seated on donkeys
parading down the main street.
Off to the vineyards I was told.
I sensed God one morning too when a bare-
footed little girl appeared.
Over she goes to a running fountain and
washes her little face.
A beautiful sight to behold.
The plane touches down at Dublin airport.
A wonderful nostalgic feeling.
Back in my own green land again.
It's so nice to go rambling, but it's so much
nicer to come home.
Arrivederci Italy.

YOUR OWN MEMORIES

TUBBERCLAIR

'In the background stands a lake peeping
through the swaying trees'.
'From where the mist comes moving slowly
carried by the gentle breeze'.
Not as poetic as Goldsmith, but verse penned
on Tubberclair Chapel.
The Chapel stands in Goldsmith country.
'Sweet Auburn loveliest village of the plane'.
Replaced now by the 'Village of the Roses'
called Glasson.
And it's not in any way deserted, but
blooming in fact.
In the little Chapel Fr. Gillooly prays
to Our Lady.
The organ playing quietly in the background.
'Our Lady is a great auld character', he once
informed me.
If the Chapel could speak what stories
it would tell.
The joy of a young couple saying 'I Do'.
The tears as an old friend says goodbye.
'Round the Church there lies a graveyard to
the memory of those gone'.
'Every headstone tells a story as we
move quietly along'.

The Spirit from the Chapel moves out into
other areas of the Parish.
The sweet sound of the marching Pipe Band.
Led by Paul of the broad smile.
Each member in step to the beat of the
side drum.
There's Girl guides and Brownies
dressed in blue.
And badminton too.
The old school house which is now a hall.
There to be used by all.
Near by stands the new school with its prize
winning gardens.
The sound of the childrens voices create
their own music at lunch break.
There's camogie for the girls and football
for the boys.
The footballers of Tubberclair created their
own bit of history.
Not because they won the junior football
final in 1967.
Because they stood up on the crossbar to try
and save a point.
Well there's no rule against it, is there?
The senior team won the county final, maybe
their first, in 1985.
They were poetry in motion that day.
What would Goldsmith say.

MICHAEL O'HEHIR

'The ball is in and the game is on'.
It was August 1985 as 1 walked with my thoughts
down O'Connell St.
Michael O'Hehir stepped up on the footpath
in front of me.
My first time to see him live so to speak.
'I mustn't miss this opportunity to speak to
the great Broadcaster'.
'Hello Michael', says I.
'Oh howya', says he as he turned around.
I felt taller than usual as we walked the
footpath together.
We discussed the following Sundays game between
Mayo and Dublin.
He gave me hope by saying that Mayo would do
better than people thought.
They did. They drew.
The replay ....
Michael was about to broadcast the match we
were discussing.
But it was not to be.
To my amazement next morning I read that he
got a stroke.
He was also getting ready to broadcast his
100th. All-Ireland Final.

A big year for him.
But that was not to be either.
The great G.A.A. voice silenced.
Would Sunday afternoon ever be the
same again.
Memories of groups huddled around the
large radio.
All ears as Michael dramatised the game.
Often more exciting than being present
at the match.
He possibly did as much for radio as he did
for the G.A.A.
'Christy Ring bends, lifts, strikes and the
ball is in the net'.
He made household names of Purcell, Ring ,
Rackard, O'Connell, Doyle, Spillane.
McKeever, Heffernan and Kehir.
The man in the box always focussed our
attention like only he could.
An Irish Sunday with Mass in the morning ,
and Michael O'Hehir after lunch.
As simple as that, you might say.
'Time ticking away now'.
'The referee looks at his watch'.
'He blows his whistle'.
'It's all over'.
Slan agus beanacht Michael.

DRAMA AT CLOGHER

There they were meeting the President
of Ireland.
Clogher Foroige club.
Tops in Ireland, no mean feat.
Their creative energy knew no bounds.
Channelled in the right direction.
Teenagers with a goal.
They had arrived.
Us older ones had our own memories.
We wandered back thirty years mentally.
The riverside players Clogher were born.
We were all eager teenagers then too.
Flowing like the little Pebble river.
The hall was roofless so we practiced our
plays in the school.
It whiled away the dark wintry evenings.
Most teenagers were Pioneers then.
No lounge bars to attract our attention.
No dances during Lent either.
So a drama group was ideal for us youth.
We got as much fun out of the rehearsals as
did our audience the play.
We always went for comedies.
The safest option for newcomers.
Any mistakes added to the comedy.

The audiences seemed to enjoy our mistakes.
We gave some good performances too.
We thought we were on Broadway sometimes.
Then we had to dismantle the stage, ourselves,
after the performance.
We knew then that Broadway was quite a
bit away still.
Gradually we went our separate ways.
Forming our own real-life dramas.
Did Shakespeare not say: 'Life is a stage and
we are all actors'.
Ours was a Macra na Feirme group.
Eugene Vahey being the leading light.
In Mike Garry we had the most natural
comedian in Ireland.
Macra gave way to Foroige.
The children in Clogher school will soon
form their own group.
The name they give it doesn't matter, so
long as they create.
Clogher is the hub.
Surrounded by the villages of Drum, Fortlawn,
Killeen, Knockboy.
Thomastown, Cloonboro. Catford, Carramore.
Lisblowick, Pollalena, Newtown, Dromore.
Images of the past, dreams of the future.
Time rolls by.
Just like the little Pebble river at Clogher.

YOUR OWN MEMORIES

_____

_____

_____

_____

_____

_____

_____

_____

_____

_____

_____

_____

_____

_____

_____

_____

_____

_____

_____

_____

_____

_____

_____

THE ALL-IRELAND FINAL

We had waited a long time for this day.
Most of us hadn't remembered the last
time it happened.
Mayo were in the All-Ireland final for the
first time in forty years.
We decorated the county in red and
green flags.
John O'Mahony was preparing the team.
Mentally, physically and psychologically.
We knew we were going to win.
We weren't biased atall atall.
We had Willie Joe not complete
without Mayo.
We had Liam McHale who didn't need to
jump atall.
Just put up one hand and take down the ball.
We had Flanagan, Browne and T.J.
And Finnerty and Durcan to make our day.
Well the great day finally arrived.
The last person to leave Mayo put out
the lights.
No doubt it would be lit up in a blaze
of glory next day.
Croke Park, Dublin, get ready we're on
our way.

My brother Brendan drove the Cork team, to
the pitch, in his coach.
Martin's driveway is choc-a-block with MO
registrations; or is it IZ?
My sister Eileen and myself take our seats
in the Hogan stand.
The Artane Boys Band are already enter-
taining the crowd.
Everybody now restless with anticipation.
The roar of the crowd tells us something
is happening.
Yes, the teams are racing on to the pitch.
The game is now in progress and Cork go
four points clear.
Willie Joe soars into the air and sends the
ball over the bar.
Finnerty rattles the net after half time.
Michael O'Muirchetaigh paints the picture
on radio.
Clearer than anything seen on T.V.
Mayo fans could be heard roaring below
in Belmullet.
If there was anybody there that is.
It was not to be our day however.
Cork edged ahead in the end.
But the experts tell us it was one of the
better All-Irelands.
Our dream goes on.

LIFE IS A MYSTERY

We sat in Dempseys lounge in Balla.
Watching Nelson Mandella walking down the
street in Johannesburg.
Set free after spending twenty five
years in prison.
We were only half concentrated on this
momentous occasion.
We were just after leaving Da to rest in
Guesdian graveyard.
With the wind whistling through the ruins
of the castle on the hill.
It was the eleventh of February 1990.
A hurricane accompanied by rain and sleet
was the order of the day.
Nelson Mandella was set free from prison
that memorable day.
John Heneghan was set free from the body.
Returned to the earth from which it came.
So fitting in a way for Da because he
loved the land.
We all have a craving for the earth I
would imagine.
I suppose death is a fact of life.
The only thing we can be sure of.
We are just on a pilgrimage
Death is a mystery.

Da dropped dead outside his home
at Donamona.
'As long as there's a breath in my body
I'll be working', he said.
True to his word he died with the yard
brush in his hands.
And his last words to my Mother: 'It will
grow again'.
Referring to the pyracanta tree from which
he broke a branch.
Does not everything grow again?
Life did grow again in the form of twin
grand-daughters that same year.
The pyracanta tree blooms on year after
year, after year.
With red berries for the birds in the
frosty Winter.
And white flowers for the bees in the long
days of summer.
It will grow again!
By the medium of television we watched
Nelson Mandella step by step.
He was unaware of what was happening in
Guesdian graveyard.
Life and death mingled together on a cold
Winter morning.
The scent of the resurrection in the wind.
Life is a mystery.

MAYNOOTH

As I write Maynooth College has just celebrated its 200th. anniversary.
Mention Maynooth and one automatically
thinks of the College.
The Seminary mostly, but now the recent
university too.
But Maynooth has other interesting
features as well.
The old castle, canal and railway station,
mill and leafy glade.
All surrounding, and forming part of, the
picturesque village.
In this Co. Kildare town I now reside.
The Seminary was set up in 1795, and has
become World famous.
The spire in the distance called me to this
college of Clerical learning.
It was a foggy wintry morning as I entered
the tree covered avenue.
'Not a sinner in sight', as the old
saying goes.
The flowers that bloom in the Spring have
gone to bed.
There's just a beautiful silence in the
Christmas time frosty fog.

As quietly as possible I open a large door
and enter a building.
I walked, not as silently as I had hoped,
down a long wide corridor.
Each step causing an echo.
Stopping quite often to view the photo frames
along the wall.
A familiar face sometimes peers out
directly at me.
'There's Padraig Staunton I went to the
national school with'.
The photo's get older as I ease myself
tranquilly along.
Marching silently backwards through years
of clerical history.
The last frame contains the class of 1938.
The Belcarra curate of my youth, Fr. Walsh,
was in that one.
His photo evoking memories of times past.
I exited as quietly as I had entered at the
other end of the building.
Trees and football pitches greeted me
at this end.
I viewed in my mind's eye all the young men
sweating it out at football.
The stillness reflecting the signs of the times.
I wander home with my thoughts.

GRAFTON STREET

Present circumstances takes me to Grafton
Street, Dublin, on a daily basis.
Is there a nicer street in the World?
As beauty is in the eye of the beholder
I suppose there is.
But Grafton Street is tops for me.
Unlike other streets there's no
rushing about.
People just out for a stroll.
No motor traffic to disturb the peace.
It's like going to the theatre too.
Music, Poetry, Song and Mime.
The Diceman is gone, but the rest carry on.
Grafton Street wouldn't be Grafton Street
without the buskers.
Streets where traffic roars by people rush
on the footpath too.
Strange Indeed!
Rush and the World rushes with you.
Where are we rushing to I wonder?
It would be hard to imagine people fighting
in Grafton Street.
All nationalities mingling together like a
big happy family.
A mass of humanity at ease and wonder.

St.Stephens Green stands at one end of
Grafton Street.
'Dublin can be heaven with coffee at eleven
and a stroll in Stephens Green'.
The tranquillity of the Green is like
paradise itself.
Children feeding ducks in the pond.
An old man having a snooze on a bench
shaded by the trees.
A young couple walking hand in hand.
At the other end stands the famous
Trinity College.
First let's branch off for a moment to the
Westbury Mall.
And a word of wisdom from Terence.
I'm sure The Provost of Trinity ponders the
diversity of life.
Glancing out his window at the crowds.
In his childhood he glanced out another
window at Cluainduane.
The rugged landscape of heather and
blackberry bushes.
A different time, a different place.
The diversity makes the beauty.
Life goes on to a different scene.
'Grafton Street's a wonderland, there's
music in the air'.
Come and meet me there.

YOUR OWN MEMORIES

GARABANDAL

I told Mick I was going to Garabandal.
'Would that be outside Belmullet by any
chance', says he.
Most people have their favourite place
of pilgrimage.
A place apart.
Mine is a little remote village by the name
of Garabandal.
High up in the Cantabrian mountains of
north-western Spain.
Of course a place of pilgrimage could be
ones back garden.
Anyway once I read it's little story I wanted
to see this place.
Our Lady made many appearances to four
young girls.
She appeared at nine pine trees, on a hill,
above the village.
She asked them to lead good lives, and visit
the Blessed Sacrament.
To make sacrifices and perform penance.
She promised that a miracle will take place
at the pines soon.
Only one girl, Conchita, knows the date.
To be announced eight days in advance.
The mountains of Spain were calling me.

So here I am at Garabandal in the cool of
a Sunday evening.
I'm standing, all alone, at the nine pine
trees in the dusk.
Down below I can just see the red roofs of
the village houses.
Everything is more or less as I imagined in
its beautiful ruggedness.
Though the little rocky path to the pines is
steeper than I thought.
The girls often ran at great speed backwards down this path.
Some extraordinary things have happened
at Garabandal.
After a little meditation and prayer I head
back down to the village.
My pilgrimage group are sitting down
to some food.
A noisy bunch now after a long day
on the coach.
The journey up the mountain was breathtaking in every sense.
Both for its beauty and the steep drop as we
zig-zagged our way up.
We are on a scenic mountain surrounded by
higher mountains.
We end our day with prayer in the little
rough-stoned chapel.

I'M OFF FOR PHILADELPHIA

My cousin Fred picked me up at the Central Railway
Station in Philadelphia.
'The City of Brotherly Love, and the Liberty Bell'.
"Hi Tom, How are you doin'?"
"Ah, not too bad Fred".
One fifth of the Philadelphia region claim Irish
ancestry; over a million people.
So I'm travelling through a most interesting city for
lots of reasons.
"Do you see that building over there?" said Fred.
"Well that's the post office where your Grand Uncle,
John Kilcourse, worked for 35 years."
I was silent for a moment thinking of the telegrams
coming from Clogher Post Office.
The telegram was the fastest means of communication
at that time, and it arrived by bicycle.
Also the Christmas card from Marie and Ed delivered
by postman Seamus McGarry.
I thought of the hardship, and adventure, John
Kilcourse went through to get here.
The tearful goodbye to his parents at Fairhill and the
trip to Queenstown Port, Cobh, Co. Cork.
'Many young men of twenty said goodbye!'
The boarding of the Baltic Ship and trip across the
broad Atlantic for America.
His arrival at Ellis Island on the 19th September 1914.

Better get back to the present now as Fred whisks me
through the countryside towards West Chester.
The Autumn trees golden leaves and the mild evening
blend in nicely with my thoughts.
"Well Fred it's taken a while for a Heneghan to reach
his cousins in America, but this is it."
"Yea Tom, I guess everything happens in its own
good time."
We reach our destination and I greet the Manning
household at their house on the little hill.
Fred's mother Kate and sisters Maureen, Jeanne and
baby give me a wonderful welcome.
Mary-Ann and her husband join us later.
We view some photos and reminisce about olden times
in Fairhill, Guesdian and Welshpool.
They tell me that the Manning side of the family comes
from Ballinahown, Co. Offaly.
An evening to ponder, think, wonder.
"You'd never guess whose piano that is," said Fred,
as I tinkle the keys.
"I'd never guess," says I.
"Well that's John McCormack's piano given to us by
his widow some years ago."
That caught my attention, and started my questions,
but that's a story for another day.
I touched the Atlantic before leaving America.
I touched it again in Mayo on my return home as I
glanced across the ocean to Philadelphia.

GAY BYRNE

While Michael O'Hehir made radio popular
he made way for Gay.
The King of Irish radio and T.V. for the
latter part of the 20th century.
It was about 1960 when we heard that Sandy
Kelly had Television.
My imagination ran wild.
Would it be really possible to see the
Flintstones moving on screen?
I had read their escapades every Sunday
in the Sunday Press.
Would it be possible to see Charles Mitchel
reading the news?
Almost beyond our comprehension.
After days of anticipation the great
moment arrived.
We invited ourselves to see the first T.V.
in the neighbourhood.
In awe we saw the Flintstones moving in
their stone-wheeled car.
And Charles Mitchel actually smiling out
at all of us.
It was an incredible moment.
Just as fascinating as we imagined it would be.
The world in our kitchen!

Then a young black-haired chap started to
appear on screen.
With a show called 'The Late-Late', but it
wasn't that late.
He complemented the late T.V. show with an
early Radio show.
The signature tune alone gave many a
person a lift.
He talked to anybody and everybody about
anything and everything.
He had the knack of making everything
sound interesting.
With a wonderful gift of speech.
Sprinkled with a good sense of humour.
His Late-Late show caused controversy at times.
Sure enough some items would have been better
left off the airwaves.
Some say he changed Ireland.
One man even suggested that he dragged it
into the 20th. century.
What ever that means.
He says, himself, that he was in the right
place at the right time.
Where there's a talent there's a means.
He was interwoven into Irish peoples lives
like no other.
Probably the best broadcaster in the world.

BALLINTUBBER ABBEY

" 'This has been a place of prayer since its
people were baptised by St. Patrick'.
'Their graves facing the east, and the rising
Sun, are symbols of their faith.'
'The Abbey that refused to die is a symbol
of their enduring hope.'
'The ruined cloisters, and Tochar Phadraig
are symbols of their faithful love.'
'These hallowed grounds invite us to share
in that faith, that hope, that love'.
'This is a place of prayer and peace'."
The above inscription greets you as you
enter Ballintubber Abbey.
I often passed this Abbey in the valley as
a youngster.
Not realizing the treasure inside.
Sometimes we don't appreciate what's on
our own doorstep.
A case of far away hills being greener.
Ballintubber Abbey was founded in 1216 by
The King of Connaught.
Put in perspective, the Abbey was 276 years
old when Columbus discovered America.
America has changed since.
Ballintubber not a lot.
Fr. Frank is balancing change without change.

Tobar Phadraig (Ballintubber) means: 'The
Townland of the Well of St. Patrick.'
Patrick arrived here by way of
Tochar Phadraig.
The ancient pilgrim path to the Reek.
Modern day pilgrims use the restored path
once more.
Church Island, out on beautiful Lough Carra,
calls one too.
Ballintubber Abbey is dedicated to the
Holy Trinity.
" *'I arise today in Power and Might.'*
'I call upon the Trinity with faith in
the Threeness'.
'And trust in the Oneness of the great
World's Maker'."
A tranquil stillness surrounds the Abbey
and all who enter here.
Remarkably Mass has been celebrated here
for close to 800 years.
Even the burning of the Abbey didn't dampen
Priest or Peoples spirit.
Shawl clad women, kneeling on the grass, in
the roofless Abbey.
Mass for the congregation, in the snowflakes,
under the dome of the sky.
Ballintubber! yes indeed, here is the 'Abbey that
refused to die'.

THE HOLY LAND

To walk where Jesus walked is the aspiration
of many.
It came my way more by chance than aspiration.
Maybe a lot of things in life are like that.
Striving for one thing receiving another.
What could be more interesting.
I'm touching down at Tel Aviv airport after a
six hour flight.
Passport control can be wearisome after a
long journey.
On to Natanya, on the Mediterranean coast,
for a good nights rest.
Next day we head north towards Caesarea;
ancient capital of Palestine.
On then to Mount Tabor, traditional site of
the Transfiguration, for Mass.
"His face shone like the Sun, and his clothes
became as white as the light".
I'm looking forward to Nazareth.
Images of Jesus in the carpentry shop.
"He will be called a Nazarene".
Not the quiet little place I imagined.
It's a hive of activity.
Down the road now a short distance to Cana.
No wedding today I'm afraid.

Israel and Palestine are the home of the Holy Land.
Together smaller than Ireland.
"Walking by the sea of Galilee, trying to set
men free".
We head for Capernaum across the water.
The engine of the boat is switched off in the
middle of the lake.
A beautiful tranquillity comes over us.
"He commanded the sea to be calm".
Up now to the mount of the Beatitudes.
"Blessed are the peacemakers".
Down again to the sea shore to the site of the
miracle of loaves and fishes.
A silent wonder among the people in the calm
of the evening.
On to the Jordan river where we witness some
baptisms taking place.
It's amazing how close all those places mentioned
are to each other.
Time to leave Galilee and head south to Jerusalem.
All along the three hour journey we view the
Jordanian mountains.
Grass is in scarce supply.
We pass Jerico near the dead sea.
Did you know that you can float in the Dead Sea?
The water thick with salt.
Night is falling; time for rest.

JERUSALEM

Continuing our Holy Land Journey.
Early in the morning we drive to the place
where Jesus was born.
"We saw his star in the east".
Bethlehem on a hazy sunny morning.
Where Mary laid the babe in a manger.
Shepherds, with their sheep, in rapt awe.
Up now the short distance to Jerusalem.
We take the old Roman road through the hills
of the Judean wilderness.
Appropriately listening to 'The Holy City' as
our coach tops the hill.
We pause at the Mount of Olives to enjoy a
panoramic view of the City.
On to Mount Zion to visit the cenacle.
We view the upper room of the last supper.
"Take this all of you and eat; this is my body
which is given up for you".
Next we visit the beautiful, art decorated, Church
of Gallicantu (Cock-crow).
We walk the Pilgrim Way down to the Garden
of Gethsemane.
After visiting the Basilica of the Agony we
cross the Kidron Valley.
Entering the old City through St. Stephen's Gate.

Jerusalem draws Jews, Christians and Muslims
by the hundred thousands.
All wanting to see this place where Solomon
built the Temple.
Where Jesus preached and died.
Where Muhammad dreamed of the Dome.
For all three Faiths the city has become a symbol
of the new Jerusalem.

"The whole Creation is groaning in one great act
of giving birth".
The Temple was built by Solomon in 950 B.C.
The Dome of the Rock was erected in 687 A.D.
We continue our own journey by joining the Jews
in prayer at the Wailing Wall.
Up then to the Temple Mount and a visit to the
Dome of the Rock.
Shoes must be removed to enter.
We begin walking the 'Way of the Cross' up the
narrow, shop-filled, streets.
Maybe the best place to be made an example of.
"Veronica wipes the face of Jesus".
On to Golgotha where Jesus was crucified.
Surprising indeed to find the Hill of Calvary
within the city.

I had a picture of a quiet hill in my mind.

"He is not here; he is risen".

Hosanna in the Highest.

THE CRANE

The Berlin Wall was coming down.
I'm sure they used a crane.
Sky scrapers being built all over the World.
Yes they use the crane.
The crane is a symbol of both the past and
the present.
The future who knows?
Then there's the crane fhada, the long necked bird,
from where the name originated.
Every house had a crane in the good
old days.
It held the pot of spuds.
It held the singing kettle.
The modern crane is building a World of
tar and cement.
It's automatically pushing the old crane out
with modern housing.
The old slipping away in spite of us.
'Time and tide waits for no one'.
The 20th. century has seen some almost
incredible achievements.
The landing of man on the Moon has to be
the most amazing.
Ger and myself watching planes landing at
Knock held its own fascination.
The crane bridges the old with the new.

That's the scene as we enter the new
Millennium.
Some would have you believe we are in
the end times.
They feel they are reading the signs of
the times.
Time will tell.
In spite of the achievements we still have
the poor, the homeless.
Cruel wars break out here and there.
Perhaps our spiritual development did not
keep up with the material.
We got carried away.
We are either in the depths of depression or
floating above the clouds.
We need God to anchor us.
Rather than the end times perhaps we are
entering new times.
A time where each individual will be respected
for her/his uniqueness.
And animals too.
And Ireland might become the 'Island of saints
and scholars' once more.
Let's pray that the vision becomes reality.
My Mother still sits beside the crane in her
open hearth fire.
Peace be with you.

YOUR OWN MEMORIES